NOTHING MORE

NOTHING MORE

SENIOR REFLECTIONS

DIANE HARPER

Published by Redemption Press, PO Box 427, Enumclaw, WA 98022.
Toll-Free (844) 2REDEEM (273-3336)

Redemption Press is honored to present this title in partnership with the author. The views expressed or implied in this work are those of the author. Redemption Press provides our imprint seal representing design excellence, creative content, and high-quality production.

The author has tried to recreate events, locales, and conversations from memories of them. In order to maintain their anonymity, in some instances the names of individuals, some identifying characteristics, and some details may have been changed, such as physical properties, occupations, and places of residence.

All Scripture, unless otherwise indicated, is taken from The Holy Bible, New International Version, © 1973, 1978, 1984, 2011 by Biblica, Inc. Used by permission. All rights reserved worldwide. Published by Zondervan, Grand Rapids, Michigan 49530 USA.

New American Standard Bible nasb 1995 (Includes Translators' Notes,) © 1960, 1962, 1963, 1968, 1971, 1972, 1973, 1975, 1977, 1995 by the Lockman Foundation, A Corporation for nonprofit, La Habra, California. All rights reserved. www.lockman.org

The Oswald Chambers quotation is taken from My Utmost for His Highest by Oswald Chambers, © 1935 by Dodd Mead & Co., renewed © 1963 by the Oswald Chambers Publications Assn., Ltd. Used by permission of Discovery House, Grand Rapids, MI 49501. All rights reserved. (7/30, 8/2)

The Glyn Evans quotation is taken from Daily with the King by Glyn Evans, © 1979 by the Moody Bible Institute of Chicago. Used by permission. (7/14)

The Beth Moore quotation is taken from James Mercy Triumphs, page 90, by Beth Moore, © 2011. Beth Moore. Published by LifeWay Press. Used by permission.

ISBN 13: 978-1-64645-506-5 (Paperback)

Library of Congress Catalog Card Number: 2021912206

CONTENTS

INTRODUCTION

I LAID OUT *SENIOR REFLECTIONS* IN THIS DEVOTIONAL BY subject. Some contain hymns and places for journaling. I also tuck in bits of history here and there, bringing remembrances of my senior journey with my husband.

We all have rich memories to share with one another. I pray you will enjoy and be encouraged as I share mine with you. The last one is yet to be written until Jesus takes me home.

Because Your lovingkindness is better than life,
My lips will praise You.
So I will bless You as long as I live;
I will lift up my hands in Your name.

Psalm 63:3–4

AGING

CARDED!

The LORD does not look at the things people look at.
People look at the outward appearance, but the LORD looks at the heart.

1 Samuel 16:7

I REMEMBER WHEN I WAS AROUND EIGHTEEN OR SO. SOME of us wanted to look older so we could go to those places that were off limits because of our age. We tried to dress and act nonchalant as we strolled into a club, praying we wouldn't be "carded." Sometimes we even used someone else's ID, hoping the one checking didn't look too closely at the picture. More often than not, we were sent on our way. And then when we turned that magic age of twenty-one, we wanted to be carded so we could flaunt that we really were old enough.

On into our thirties, we wanted to be carded because we hoped we looked younger than we really were. The years rolled by, and we reached the various ages of discounts for senior citizens. Sometimes we had to show our ID to prove we were old enough for the discount. That felt good! Then came the Medicare age of sixty-five. But the shocker came the day when we didn't ask for the senior discount—we were just given it automatically!

Our outer appearance seems to haunt us, one way or another, for our entire lives. Some go to extremes to appear either older or younger than they really are. Men and women travel down the road of dyeing hair, wearing hair pieces, taking trips to the gym and spa, wearing various styles of clothes, getting face-lifts, and wearing more or less makeup. On and on it goes.

So where does this leave us? Do we buy into all the hype of the outer appearance, or do we listen to God? Scripture has much to say on what really matters to God, which of course is the condition of the heart, our relationship to Him. Those of us who are seniors know that gray hair is a plus in God's economy: "A gray head is a crown of glory; it is found in the way of righteousness" (Proverbs 16:31). Proverbs 20:29 says, "The glory of young men is their strength, gray hair is the splendor of the old." We don't read anywhere in Scripture where Noah, Moses, Abraham, Samuel, John, or even Sarah were concerned about their appearance as they aged. Their advanced years never stopped them from doing great things for God!

We do want to take care of ourselves, not abusing our bodies. We do need to be neat and clean, but there must be a balance. Too much focus on our appearance is unhealthy.

God knows our age. He honors age and aging. But He also has a plan for each one of us at this place in our senior years.

THOUGHT FOR THE DAY

The righteous will flourish like the palm tree
They will still bear fruit in old age

Psalm 92:12–14

Father God, sometimes this aging process is frustrating, and sometimes it is painful. Help me follow Your plan with joy, trusting You all the way. Amen.

Do you know what His plan is for you right now, whatever age you are? Record your thoughts.

OLD IN '09

Do not cast me away when I am old;
Do not forsake me when my strength is gone.

Psalm 71:9

AS I WROTE THIS AT THE END OF 2009 AND NOW AM WRITING in 2020, I have come to the realization that my husband and I have become really old. Some areas of our physical bodies do not work the way they did last year at this time. We thought we were dealing with the aging process, but this year all the denial that we are not *that* old has been stripped away. This creeping process is no longer creeping. The "over the hill" expression is sending us speeding down the other side. Last year's aches and pains seemed to have doubled now. After shoveling a foot of snow, we know we are old!

The departure of physical strength and stamina is hard enough to deal with, but my mental attitude concerns me more. When I was younger, I would wince at grumpy, set-in-their-ways senior citizens. They were always complaining about some health issues, the cost of everything, the state of the world, the confusing technology. But now I find myself whining and mumbling over the same things. And boy did I cringe the other day when my husband said he was set in his ways.

It is important to keep our minds active as our body declines. There is no excuse for my husband and me to not be as mentally engaged as possible. A former 98-year-old neighbor, who had many health issues, wrote four books after the age of 90. In the last week of his life, he was still trading on the stock market. There is so much out there to keep us mentally active so that we don't turn into those grumpy old people. We can't do anything about the old, but we sure can do something about the grumpy!

The aging process is part of God's plan, whether we like it or not. Instead of complaining about what we can't do anymore, we need to ask God to show us what we *can* do. There is much He has changed in our life to this point. Maybe that hike to the top of a thirteen-thousand-foot mountain won't happen. And next year we will have to hire a younger body to shovel our walk. A friend said she had to buy long sleeves because her upper arms were in ruins. (Mine are in the same state.)

The other morning in my quiet time, I opened God's Word to Isaiah 46:4. "Even to your old age, I will be the same, and even to your graying years I will bear you! I have done it, and I will carry you; And I will bear you and I will deliver you" (NASB). This is just one of the many promises that He will take care of us.

We can do nothing without Him. We couldn't in our youth, and we can't now. These senior years are for drawing us into a closer, more intimate relationship with our Savior. Many of life's struggles are behind us. We are becoming more and more dependent on Him; our denial is over. We are not 20, 30, 40, 50, 60, or . . . anymore. Let's draw close to Him, stop stressing over what is behind us, and see what new and exciting things He has planned.

THOUGHT FOR THE DAY

Do not call to mind the former things,
Or ponder things of the past.
Behold I will do something new,
Now it will spring forth;
Will you not be aware of it?
I will even make a roadway
in the wilderness, Rivers in the desert.

Isaiah 43:18–19 NASB

Father God, day by day make me aware of new things You desire to do in me and through me. Amen.

NOW WHAT?

But now, Lord, what do I look for?
My hope is in you.
Psalm 39:7

WELL, HERE I AM, AND MAYBE YOU ARE TOO, ON THE OTHER side of that magic age of sixty-five; or I guess you could say I'm a full-fledged senior citizen, qualifying for everything, no other milestone needing to be reached. But now what?

What do You have planned for me now, Father God? So many struggles are behind me, but many lie ahead, each of a different nature. And I just seem to be waiting—for what, I don't know. So much of what I thought I wanted to do—some big thing for God—I realize is now behind me. Denial is over. I'm not going to be a full-time missionary in the jungles somewhere. For me, that would have been a big thing for God. It's just not reality, and obviously, it is not what God had planned for my life anyway. "The mind of man plans his way, but the LORD directs his steps" Proverbs 16:9 (NASB). For me, I am always going to do such and such next year. It's not that I haven't reached some of the goals I have worked for, but I still feel there is more to come, much more. And the older I get, the least significant task appears to be the meaning of my days. So, I am waiting.

But am I being distracted by waiting while God puts something He wants me to do right in front of me? I also realize that the every-day duties bring glory to God. There is opportunity to serve family, neighbors, fellow Christians, and the homeless I encounter. I am aware of these things, and while they seem small to me, they are big to God.

Matthew 25:35–40 reminds us to feed the hungry, clothe the naked, invite the stranger in, and visit the sick and those in prison: "The King will reply, 'Truly I tell you, whatever you did for one of the least of these brothers and sisters, you did it for me'" (vs. 40).

THOUGHT FOR THE DAY

What am I waiting for?

Father God, I always seem to need reminders to stop waiting for some big thing to do for You. Show me the small things that You are calling me to do every day. May I always be about Your business in the big and the small. Amen.

What is God calling you to do today that you don't think is important?

WHILE I SLEPT

When you lie down, you will not be afraid;
when you lie down, your sleep will be sweet.

Proverbs 3:24

WHEN DID THAT HAPPEN? I LOOK CLOSER IN THE MIRROR, and I am convinced that spot wasn't there yesterday. Another old age spot to add to my collection! God must have put it there while I slept. Some men and women never get them, while I seem to have moved from zits to old age spots. *When did that happen?*

Do you ever really think about all God does while we sleep? Many of the physical changes and bodily processes that God has created go on while we sleep. It is mind-boggling. The sleep we need to be rejuvenated is obvious, but even that tiny cut that bothered us the day before is much better the next morning. However, while we sleep, I do wish the aging process could be reversed!

To look at the bigger picture, Scripture tells us other things our awesome God does while we sleep. As seniors, we sometimes have trouble sleeping. We know too much about all the problems and dangers that could occur. Especially if we live alone we may have more fears and worries about if someone tried to break in or if we fall and can't call for help. Psalm 4:8 is a verse to hang onto during those times: "In peace I will lie down and sleep, for you alone, LORD, make me to dwell in safety."

We all have those nights when sleep is elusive. If we could just fall asleep as quickly as we did in front of the television! We toss and turn, can't get comfortable, are in pain, or our minds are racing with a million to-do's. And whether awake or finally asleep, Psalm 42:8 is such a comfort: "By day the LORD directs his love, at night his song is with me—a prayer to the God of my life." It is a wonderful reminder of God's abiding presence in our waking and sleeping hours.

An even bigger picture is in another Psalm where we are told by God, who keeps Israel: "He will not allow your foot to slip; He who keeps you will not slumber. Behold, He who keeps Israel Will neither slumber nor sleep" (Psalm 121:3–4). He never sleeps as He keeps the whole world. It all goes according to His plan. He even guards the vineyard at night (Isaiah 27:3).

When I focus on Him and His Word at bedtime, He will speak to my mind while I sleep. "I will praise the LORD, who counseled me; even at night my heart instructs me" (Psalm 16:7).

THOUGHT FOR THE DAY

His eye is on the sparrow, and I know He watches me.
—Civilla D. Martin (1866–1948)

Father God, Your awesomeness blows me away. To know everything, even when the sparrow falls and when I'm sleeping. If I am sleeping peacefully, or if I am in turmoil, You are there. Thank You. Amen.

GOD'S GIFTS

YOU'VE GOT TO BE TOUGH!

I am the vine, you are the branches. If you remain in me and I in you, you will bear much fruit; apart from me you can do nothing.

John 15:5

GREAT BASIN NATIONAL PARK, ON THE BORDER OF NEVADA and Utah, is home to the bristlecone pine trees. They are found in the elevations between 9,500 and 11,000 feet and grow on the slopes of Mt. Wheeler, Nevada's second highest mountain of 13,063 feet. These trees can live two thousand to three thousand years, although they don't all live to that ripe old age. The oldest grow near the tree line where survival is the most difficult, with adversity fostering life. They grow very slowly, one branch at a time. Their needles live up to forty years. As you can imagine, the weather at that altitude challenges all forms of life. Whether tree or man, you've got to be tough to live there.

We want to be tough, still standing strong at the end of our life after the storms, the trials and testings. But *tough* doesn't happen on our own, no matter how much we feel in control or think we will be able to come through each crisis we face. Only God gives the strength, the toughness, to go through the suffering and devastating losses we will experience. How do we avail ourselves of God's strength and power in times of need? Certainly, not by fighting against it with a "why me" attitude, nor by trying in our own strength to pull through. Total surrender to God is the only answer. We must state, as Paul does in 2 Corinthians 12:10b, ". . . for when I am weak, then I am strong."

In Acts 14 we have the story of the man lame from his mother's womb. Paul sees that he has the faith to be healed and commands him to stand to his feet (vs. 10). The man physically weak was strong in his faith.

You have to be tough when you walk with the Lord, not in your own strength, but with a toughness that says, "I know I stand because of Him and His life in me."

THOUGHT FOR THE DAY

Are you like a bristlecone pine?

Father God, You are with me through every storm I will face in this life. I will be stronger after each storm because You have brought me through. Amen.

ADOPTION LEGACY

But when the fullness of the time came,
God sent forth His Son, born of a woman, born under the Law,
so that He might redeem those who were under the Law,
that we might receive adoption as sons.
Galatians 4:4–5 NASB

EVEN AS A CHILD, I WANTED TO MOTHER MANY CHILDREN. My plan was to birth some and adopt some. A few years into our marriage, we had our first child, Emily. When she was about six months old, the Lord laid on our hearts the desire to be foster parents. Our first foster child came the next year, followed by the birth of our son, Andrew. Many more foster children followed over the years, interspersed with the adoption of Chelsea, Michael, and Robert. After all these years, it is hard to imagine that I did not birth each of them. God has infused His Spirit into theirs and ours. We are truly parents and children.

In Bible history, God's story, many were adopted. Moses was certainly one of God's major adoption plans. Esther was raised by her uncle, Mordecai. God's destiny for her was to save her people from annihilation. King David took Mephibosheth, Johnathan's son, into his family. Ruth not only embraced her mother-in-law, Naomi, as her mother, but she also took Naomi's God as her God—no blood ties, just spirit infusion. Knowing the history of these adoptions, we see the great significance of God's plan.

Our daughter married a man who also was adopted. They have, in turn, adopted three children. All ten of our grandchildren and two great-grandchildren are from our adopted children. As our family's future unfolds, God's design will be revealed for each of them.

The adoption legacy in our family is like God's family. We are adopted sons and daughters of the King; we are princes and princesses. Paul tells us in Romans 8:15, "The Spirit you received does not make you slaves, so that you live in fear again; rather, the Spirit you received brought about your adoption to sonship. And by him we cry, '*Abba*, Father!'" (Daddy). And in Ephesians 1:5, Paul says, " he predestined us for adoption to sonship through Jesus Christ, in accordance with his pleasure and will " I truly believe the spirit is thicker than blood.

THOUGHT FOR THE DAY

We can call the Creator of all, "Daddy"!

Abba Father, you have infused us all into your family. We are truly your children, and we are forever grateful. Amen.

What are your feelings about adoption? Does it make a difference knowing that you are adopted by God? Record your thoughts.

IN REMEMBRANCE

Remember your leaders, who spoke the word of God to you.
Consider the outcome of their way of life and imitate their faith.
Hebrews 13:7

SOME OF MY CHILDREN, THE DAUGHTERS ESPECIALLY, think their mom's life is too cluttered with knick-knacks. What they don't realize is that after seventy-plus years of life, every item has a story, a memory. Most are gifts from loved ones, all special and unique. Many are handmade things from children and grandchildren.

A milk glass vase and basket from a favorite aunt not only reminds me of her, but floods me with memories of how important she was to me as I was growing up. The red and clear glass candy dish was always filled with those giant gumdrops at my grandmother's house. She always made sure there were licorice ones just for me. When I see that candy dish on my shelf, I am reminded of a grandmother who loved me very much in many different ways.

Gifts from the hands of my children are precious to me—the pottery coffee mugs with faces created in middle school, the tiny glass bottle with dried flowers, a cross fashioned with burnt matches, a tile with a stick house glued on it, and a manger scene made with Popsicle sticks—are just a few of these gifts from children. All of these knick-knacks bring with them stories and memories. And when I see them, I can say with Paul, "I thank my God every time I remember you" (Philippians 1:3).

We have these mementos of loved ones whether they are here now or have passed on. Even though we have never seen Jesus in the flesh, we know He lived and walked on this earth by historical evidence. Today we have reminders of Jesus everywhere in physical things we can touch and feel. Every word of Scripture brings God to us. "For everything that was written in the past was written to teach us, so that through the endurance taught in the Scriptures and the encouragement they provide we might have hope" (Romans 15:4).

The observance of communion comes to us from the lips of Jesus as we celebrate His sacrifice for us in a physical partaking of the bread and the wine (Luke 22:19–20). Like the candy dish that brings my grandmother's face before me, so will the simple everyday occurrences and things we see—such as a smile of a baby or a daffodil opening to the sun—show us Jesus.

THOUGHT FOR THE DAY

And can it be that I should gain
An int'rest in the Savior's blood?
Died He for me, who caused His pain?
For me, who Him to death pursued?
Amazing love! How can it be
That thou my God, shouldst die for me?
—Charles Wesley (1707–1780)

Father God, we see crosses everywhere, many as decorative items. May every cross I see show me the wood and the blood of Your amazing love! Amen.

BLOOD WORK

In him we have redemption through his blood,
the forgiveness of sins,
in accordance with the riches of God's grace
that he lavished on us.

Ephesians 1:7–8

MY HUSBAND AND I HAVE COMPLETED OUR BLOOD WORK for the year. Our doctor requires this every year, or more frequently as needed. It is amazing to me that a small vial of blood can tell the doctor many things about how our bodies are working, or not working. If we are on any medications, the blood work can reveal whether or not the dosage is correct. Does it need to be increased or decreased, or is it even the right drug? And every year we hold our breath hoping we have taken care of ourselves so cholesterol and triglyceride levels are in the proper range. And of course, we pray for no abnormalities.

Blood is life. We cannot live without it, physically or spiritually. Before Christ came, there could be no forgiveness without the shedding of blood, which is referred to in the animal sacrifice of Hebrews 9:22. But after Jesus came, this practice was no longer needed. Christ's sacrifice of His blood on the cross covered every single one of us who belongs to Him. "But now in Christ Jesus you who were far away have been brought near by the blood of Christ" (Ephesians 2:13). When He becomes our Savior and our Lord, His blood washes us clean. We are forgiven and set free from sin and death.

Here are a few lines from three hymns of long ago that say it all.

What can wash away my sin?
Nothing but the blood of Jesus.
—Robert Lowry (1826–1899)

Have you been to Jesus
For the cleansing Power?
Are you washed in the blood of the Lamb?
—Elisha A. Hoffman (1839–1929)

Would you be free from your burden of sin?
There's power in the blood,
Power in the blood.
—Lewis E. Jones (1865–1936)

THOUGHT FOR THE DAY

It is amazing how the shed blood of one sinless Man atones for us, now and forever.

Father God, where would I be without Jesus's blood? Most certainly lost and dead in my sins. Thank You a thousand times over for His blood. Amen.

ABIDING

HIS HOUSE

One thing I ask from the LORD, this only do I seek: that I may dwell in the house of the LORD all the days of my life, to gaze on the beauty of the LORD and to seek him in his temple.

Psalm 27:4

"LORD, I LOVE THE HOUSE WHERE YOU LIVE, THE PLACE where Your glory dwells" (Psalm 26:8). I love my church! We have been blessed with a beautiful building to gather in and worship as the body of Christ. But we are the church wherever we meet—a beautiful sanctuary, a storefront, a house church, or anywhere the people of God get together. Many Scriptures talk about God's house, His temple, His tabernacle. Psalm 65:4 tells us how blessed we are to go into His temple: "Blessed are those you choose and bring near to live in your courts. We are filled with the good things of your house, of your holy temple." Psalm 84:4 says, "Blessed are those who dwell in your house; they are ever praising you." All these verses of the psalmist echo my feelings about being in God's house.

I recently came across a hymn written in the sixteen hundreds. The words struck me about how meaningful it is to *go* into God's house. It's not that we don't encounter God everywhere, but it is the action taken to meet in His house with His people that He has commanded us to do. In Matthew 16:18, Jesus tells Peter, "And I tell you that you are Peter, and on this rock I will build my church, and the gates of Hades will not overcome it." Christ's authority as head of the church indicates that, when you cease to be part of the church, you are, therefore, rejecting Christ's authority over you. The New Testament tells us this in Hebrews 10:24–25, "And let us consider how we may spur one another on toward love and good deeds, not giving up meeting together, as some are in the habit of doing, but encouraging one another—and all the more as you see the Day approaching."

Many Christians don't go to church anymore. How sad to miss the blessing of fellowship with God our Father and His family, together in His house. "We who had sweet fellowship together, Walked in the house of God in the throng" (Psalm 55:14 NASB).

We cannot be part of His church and the Kingdom of God here on earth by watching preachers on TV or the Internet, or reading messages on Facebook! We need each other. We need to be accountable or we drift away from God and become one with the world.

> Open now the gates of beauty, Zion let me enter there,
> Where my soul in joyful duty, Waits on Him who answers prayer:
> O how blessed is this place, Filled with solace, light and grace.
>
> Here, O God, I come before Thee, Come Thou also down to me;
> Where we find Thee and adore Thee, There a heaven on earth must be:
> To my heart O enter Thou, Let it be Thy temple now.
>
> Here Thy praise is gladly chanted, Here Thy seed is duly sown;
> Let my soul, where it is planted, Bring forth precious sheaves alone:
> So that all I hear may be, Fruitful unto life in me.
>
> Thou my faith increase and quicken, Let me keep Thy gift divine;
> Howsoe'er temptations thicken, May Thy word still o'er me shine,
> As my guiding star through life, As my comfort in my strife.
>
> Speak, O God, and I will hear Thee, Let Thy will be done indeed:
> May I undisturbed draw near Thee, While Thou dost Thy people feed;
> Here of life the fountain flows, Here is balm for all our woes.
>
> —Joachim Neander (1650–1680)

THOUGHT FOR THE DAY

They devoted themselves to the apostles' teaching and to fellowship, to the breaking of bread and to prayer.

Acts 2:42

Father God, may Your church, Your body of believers, always be my home with You. Amen.

Are you an active member of a body of believers? If not, why not?

FOR SUCH
A TIME AS THIS

But the eyes of the LORD are on those who fear him,
on those whose hope is in his unfailing love,
to deliver them from death and keep them alive in famine.
Psalm 33:18–19

MARCH 20, 2020. NOW, AS I WRITE THIS DEVOTION, THE world has come to an almost standstill. We are in the crisis of a pandemic. We still have food, gas, essentials for survival, and the technological means to communicate with one another without physical contact. We are confined to our homes as much as possible. In some ways, we are "living off the grid," except we still have Wi-Fi. On the news, we hear the count of new confirmed cases and deaths. Countries have closed their borders. In the Scripture above, we could change the word "famine" to "pandemic." God forbid that it would come to a famine worldwide. Bottom line, we have no idea how long this will last.

As God's people, how are we reacting to something we have never experienced before? Are we full of fear? Stockpiling as much of everything possible? If you are not working because your place of work closed, are you panicked about how you are going to pay your bills? As the economy crashes, what are we to do?

We go to God's Word. If we go back to Old Testament times, we can find how God brought His people through similar circumstances. In Nehemiah 9:20–21, the people are reminded of their escape from

Egypt and how God had "their backs" the entire time in spite of their disobedience. Nehemiah recalls for them that in their forty-year trek across the desert, He provided food that never ran out, water out of rocks, and clothes and shoes that never wore out.

He is still the same God today who loves and cares for His people. So, as we go through these scary, very uncertain times, who else can we place our trust in but the God of ALL? He will never leave us nor forsake us. He will carry us through this pandemic and whatever comes next.

Let us never forget God allows these things to happen for a reason. We have walked away from Him as a nation and have been disobedient, just as God's chosen people did so long ago.

THOUGHT FOR THE DAY

We wait in hope for the LORD; he is our help and our shield. In him our hearts rejoice, for we trust in his holy name. May your unfailing love be with us, LORD, even as we put our hope in you.

Psalm 33:20–22

Abba Father, I run to You in times such as these. We who trust in You must reach out to those who are so afraid and bring the hope of our God to them—for such a time as this. Amen.

LIGHT

*I am the light of the world. Whoever follows me will
never walk in darkness, but will have the light of life.*

John 8:12

THE LIGHT THAT COMES IN MY KITCHEN WINDOW AND
plays on the table changes with the seasons. I notice things like that
now that I'm retired and not rushing here and there, too busy to notice.
The light in the fall flutters with images of leaves on the wall, bringing
a touch of sadness, hinting at the winter barrenness soon to come. The
high desert sunlight in winter comes blindingly in at another angle,
brilliantly bright, the sky a shocking blue.

Another thing I notice these days is the difference between the
light of the sun and that of an electric bulb. When the sun is illumi-
nating the room, the lamplight in the corner pales into insignificance.

When Christ walked this earth, His presence flooded light into
the darkness of evil. A violent, demon-possessed man saw Jesus from
a distance and ran up to Him, crying out with a loud voice: "What do
you want with me, Jesus, Son of the most high God?" (Mark 5:7b). The
light of Jesus was recognized immediately by this demon of darkness.
The conflict arises because, as Jesus says, "This is the verdict: Light
has come into the world, but people loved darkness instead of light
because their deeds were evil" (John 3:19).

Because we have His life living in us, we are now to bring His
life-giving light to those in the dark around us. Jesus tells us we are
the light of the world: "In the same way, let your light shine before

others, that they may see your good deeds and glorify your Father in heaven" (Matthew 5:16). Paul reminds us in Ephesians, "For you were once darkness, but now you are the light in the Lord. Live as children of light " (5:8). But John has a warning for us in 1 John 2:9, "Anyone who claims to be in the light but hates a brother or sister is still in the darkness."

It is so easy to be full of righteousness at church and in our Christian circles, but to live full of darkness with our words and actions when we are in the world. If His life is in us as we claim it is, we must allow that light to shine forth in every part of our lives.

THOUGHT FOR THE DAY

O send out Your light and Your truth, let them lead me;
Let them bring me to Your holy hill,
And to Your dwelling places.

Psalm 43:3 NASB

Jesus, shine Your light into those dark places of my life so that I will not be blinded by the darkness. Bring forth Your light through me to others. Amen.

THE PERFECT FIT

*Do not conform to the pattern of this world, but be transformed
by the renewing of your mind. Then you will be able to test
and approve what God's will is—his good, pleasing and perfect will.*

Romans 12:2

SO MANY CATCHPHRASES THESE DAYS ARE USED IN DIFFER-
ent ways. This one as a title of a magazine article caught my eye: "The
Perfect Fit." I believe it referred to a house and the people who would
live there. There is also the perfect fit for clothes, the car you drive,
your job, and a multitude of other ways this phrase is used to make
you change to fit whatever is being promoted and popular.

But what about God's fit for us? Will we be willing to change,
to obey His call? Scripture shows us that many were called to be that
perfect fit for a specific situation. The others around them thought,
"You've got to be kidding!" Moses didn't think he was the man to
deliver the Hebrews from Egypt (Exodus 3). David's family was
astounded when Samuel anointed the shepherd boy as future king of
Israel (2 Samuel 16). I'm sure the prophets Isaiah and Jeremiah were
not convinced they were the perfect fit when they found themselves in
desperate situations such as walking around naked (Isaiah 20) or weep-
ing in despair for years (Jeremiah 11). But they were faithful to obey.

The perfect fit can change us as we travel life's journey. The job or
passion we had for years doesn't work for us anymore. Music was my
life and passion for so long that I just assumed it would always be that
way. Then God led me into missions, through short-term mission trips,

and deacon of missions for our church. Who would have thought? In our senior years, God doesn't retire us. He redirects us, and that may come as a shock!

So where does that leave us many years down the road . . . set in our ways or routines, resistant to change? It should lead us to our knees, seeking to discover what God's perfect fit is for us now. Maybe, just maybe, it may only be for today.

THOUGHT FOR THE DAY

Father, Your fit is always perfect.

Father God, You came to us as a baby, born in a stable. The world could not see that as a perfect fit, but it was. Wherever You put me is Your perfect fit for me. May I accept it and rejoice in it. Amen.

What is God's perfect fit for you now? Is this where you thought you would be? Are you in agreement or grumbling about where God has you?

CHANGES

LOOKING BACK

You have heard these things; look at them all.
Will you not admit them?
From now on I will tell you of new things,
of hidden things unknown to you.

Isaiah 48:6

IT WAS HARD TO LET GO OF THE FAMILY HOME. THIRTY years and five children later, we realized it was time for a smaller house and yard. The first time we put the house on the market, it didn't sell. No problem, our son and daughter-in-law moved in, planning to buy it. The house would stay in the family, with our son carrying on the legacy of the house we all loved. It was even more special when their first child was born while they were living there. But then they decided they wanted a new house, a place to make their own memories.

Once again, the house went on the market, and the struggle began when it didn't sell. Should we move back in? We were still so emotionally attached. But God had a plan to rent the house, which we said we would never do. Our new young adult pastor moved into town and needed a place for his family, close to church and the university. But after a year and a half, they realized the house and yard were too large for them.

Back on the market our beloved house went, and this time it sold in just a few days! A young family bought it. They had two children and one on the way.

Looking back, as we so often do, we can see God's perfect plan in so many instances and experiences of our lives. Why didn't it sell the first time? Now we can see why. We learned many lessons from this experience—letting go when we need to move on to something new God has planned for us, trusting God that His ways are not our ways, and the blessings He has for others when we let go. The young family that bought the house loves it. The owner's sister lives across the street, and they know others in the neighborhood. And they know our children! God answered our prayers as this is what we had prayed for—a family to be blessed in that house as we had been blessed.

Looking back over all this has been good because God is good, all the time. His plan is always best.

THOUGHT FOR THE DAY

but one thing I do: forgetting what lies behind
and reaching forward to what lies ahead

Philippians 3:13b NASB

Father God, what I would have missed if You had sold the house the first and second times! Thank You for doing it Your way. It is always best. Amen.

Can you recall an incident in your life where God's timing proved to be the greater blessing?

I DID NOT KNOW

Sing to him a new song;
Play skillfully with a shout of joy.

Psalm 33:3

I REALLY DID NOT KNOW HOW HARD IT WOULD BE TO LET go of the house.

We lived in one house for over thirty years, raising five children of our own and many foster children within its walls and yard. As we became empty nesters, we realized the folly of living in three thousand square feet on a quarter of an acre—just the two of us with our aging bodies. I had always said I would like to live somewhere else—city, state, country—but our downsizing to a smaller house came just two miles away. I was ready for a change, or so I thought.

The downturn in the economy came upon us—the foreclosures and short sales—and our house did not sell. Our son and daughter-in-law moved in, renting to buy. Perfect! The house stayed in the family, with no emotional closure needed.

But with all the opportunity to get a good deal on a house, our children decided they wanted a house of their own to make new memories. They also wanted a house newer than thirty-five years old.

So once again our house went on the market. Every time we went over there to make sure all was move-in ready, I exclaimed loudly, verbally, and in my heart, "I'm home!" Do you see a problem here? I sure do.

I want God to change whatever needs changing in my life, spiritually and physically. When I go with His plan and am obedient, I must move into the change fully. I should not look back with longing, but only with memories. We had so many memories there: the basement filled with church youth, our daughter's engagement party, our twenty-fifth anniversary, Bible studies, potluck dinners, and all the family times, happy and sad. I need now to thank Him for the blessing of that wonderful home and that His presence dwells there still, to bless others.

THOUGHT FOR THE DAY

See, the former things have taken place,
and new things I declare; before they spring into being
I announce them to you.

Isaiah 42:9

Father God, make me aware if I'm holding on when I need to let go and move on with You into the new. Amen.

Are you hanging on to something that is preventing you from moving forward? Record your thoughts.

MANY HAVE FLOWN

But we do not want you to be uninformed, brethren, about those who are asleep,
so that you will not grieve as do the rest who have no hope.
For we believe that Jesus died and rose again, even so, God will bring
with Him those who have fallen asleep in Jesus.
1 Thessalonians 4:13–14 NASB

IN A NOVEL I READ RECENTLY, THE JEWISH PEOPLE OF BIBLE times expressed one's passing on in two different ways. The angel of death had visited or passed over, taking that person's life. The other expression was that the person had flown away, which feels more positive, like one given wings to fly to heaven, releasing one from this earthbound prison of sickness, worries, and problems of all sorts.

In the last nine months, many in our body of believers have flown away. Both men and women have lost their beloved mates of thirty or more years. What brings it home to me is they are all in our age group, the sixties, too soon by our estimation. The blessing is that they are all now with the Lord forever. For some, the flight home was expected—a terminal illness just waiting for permission to fly—and for the others, it was an unexpected takeoff!

For those of us that are left behind, we know that God's promises of comfort and strength are waiting for us. But having been close to those who have lost their mates, and me still being blessed with mine, I'm wondering many things. *Will I fly away before him? Will it be a sudden departure, or a long-suffering one for either of us? Will I be angry at God if he goes first? How will I cope in those times of loneliness?* These questions and many more have filled my mind as each person has passed on.

When we look at someone else's loss, we can't say that we could never handle it in the way they did. I was amazed and blessed when our pastor, whose wife was taken suddenly, stood before us and shared his heart as a testimony of God's grace. As he came to the platform to speak at the celebration of her life, he said, "I'm always on the other side of this officiating; I don't know if I will make it through." He shared about their marriage, her service to the Master and many amusing sidelines. She was very competitive when they played games. Our pastor said he knew what she will say when he gets to heaven. "See, I win. I got here first!" The weeks following showed us our pastor's relationship with the Lord, his deep abiding love and trust that carried him through the journey of shock and grief. His testimony to us displayed that God's grace is sufficient for the moment, day, and circumstance. His grace will be there for us, to carry us, when our loved one has flown away.

So many hymns of years ago can bring comfort for times like this. Here is one of them.

THOUGHT FOR THE DAY

"He Giveth More Grace"

He giveth more grace when the burdens grow greater;
He sendeth more strength when the hours increase.
To added affliction He addeth more mercy;
To multiplied trials, His multiplied peace.

When we have exhausted our store of endurance,
When our strength has failed ere the day half done,
When we reach the end of our hoarded resources,
Our Father's full giving is only begun.

Refrain:
His love has no limit; His grace no measure.
His power no boundary known unto men.
For out of His infinite riches in Jesus,
He giveth and giveth again!

—Annie Johnson Flint (1866–1932)

Father God, may I be ready to fly away to You! Amen.

IT IS WHAT IT IS

Jesus Christ is the same yesterday and today and forever.
Hebrews 13:8

THE BRITS SAY "FANTASTIC," AND WE SAY "AWESOME" TO emphasize something positive. "Whatever" seems to have worn out its welcome. Today I hear "It is what it is" beginning to gain popularity. This statement has several sides to it. There are some things in this life that just are and won't be changed until God decides it is time. But changes are on a continuing path of transformation. Some are slow, and others move at breakneck speed.

As a senior citizen, this speed can be alarming. I was ten when we bought our first television. Now it just isn't television—it's high-definition, and you can't buy anything else. We had one phone that sat in a little alcove in the kitchen. The technology of computers and cell phones is mind-boggling. When you go to purchase a cell phone, the clerks look at you as if you have lost your mind when you say you just want a phone that works as a phone and nothing more.

Sometimes it is hard for us seniors to embrace all this technology. Our children and grandchildren have grown up with it and haven't known anything else. I don't believe it is because we don't have the intelligence to grasp it all, but maybe we see some of the shortfalls, even dangers, of jumping on the bandwagon, embracing it without a closer look.

However, we do need to weigh all of it in what is truly a tool to bring God glory and further His kingdom. We should consider to what extent—texting, blogging, Facebook, tweeting—is taking time away from Him and time in His Word. We can connect with anyone anywhere in the world at any time. Our children, who live all over the country, can stay in touch with one another, instantly. But is that connection intimate, or is it meaningless chatter? How much time is taken up as we engage in games, silly pictures, and comments? How many face-to-face, or even voice-to-voice, relationships have been relegated to a text comment or Facebook post?

God has blessed us beyond belief in gifting man's mind to give us medical and communication technology to make our lives better. But it all needs to be measured in the light of this question: "Are we using it, or is it using us?" As we use each one of these tools, let us ask ourselves this: "Are we bringing God glory?" Is this not our purpose in all we do?

THOUGHT FOR THE DAY

*In the morning, LORD, you hear my voice; in the morning
I lay my requests before you and wait expectantly.*

Psalm 5:3

Father God, may I always put You, and my time with You, first. May the tech stuff not distract me from hearing You. Amen.

BACKWARD
AND FORWARD

Therefore we do not lose heart. Though outwardly we are wasting away,
yet inwardly we are being renewed day by day.
2 Corinthians 4:16

BACKWARD AND FORWARD—THAT IS THE PREDICAMENT where I now find myself in my advancing years. It is all wrapped up in those words—change, adjust, just "go with the flow." I know physically I will never be as I was, and that grieves me. There is so much I can't do physically anymore. So, in that respect, I feel like I'm going backward. I see in my future a wheelchair and my dear husband having to do everything for me. The apostle Paul states in 2 Corinthians that our physical bodies are decaying, or in my case, falling apart. But then he says we are not to lose heart. The only way I won't lose heart is to cling to Jesus.

Paul says we are being renewed day by day in our inner man. Part of my inner man is my mind, and so far, it is still functioning normally. But here I struggle, too. The changes in just the last decade have occurred with a swiftness that has left me in the dust. The technological advancements leave me so frustrated and angry. I feel like I'm being forced to fall in line to do everything online and through my cell phone. And if I don't want to—too bad, I lose. It is what it is, and I must change, adjust, go with the flow.

So, how do I open my mind to all this, get rid of my bad attitude, and embrace it all? Once again, Paul has the answer in Romans 12:2: "Do not conform to the pattern of this world, but be transformed by the renewing of your mind. Then you will be able to test and prove what God's will is—his good, pleasing and perfect will." If tech stuff is leading me away from God, then that is where I say "stop." But I know that a countless number of people have come to Christ because of all the technological advances—the gospel going out instantly and worldwide in multiple languages. God gave man the brains to develop it all. We must use it for His glory.

So where does that leave me? It leaves me in His presence to discover His will for me in all this confusion. How far does He want me to go in embracing technology? I must ask the Holy Spirit to teach me how to use my laptop, iPad, and cell phone to bring Him glory.

THOUGHT FOR THE DAY

May we embrace Your changes, Father God.

Abba Father, Your child is fighting the inevitable changes that are happening. Please give me wisdom and much understanding as I wade through these technological waters. Amen.

RELATIONSHIPS

TO SERVE OR
BE SERVED?

For even the Son of Man did not come to be served, but to serve,
and to give His life a ransom for many.

Mark 10:45

THERE WAS A SAYING IN THE NINETIES THAT ASKED THE question, "What would Jesus do?" You would see this displayed by the letters "WWJD" on everything from bracelets, posters, devotionals, and even the subject of a novel. This saying covers what we should ask ourselves when we are called to serve in some way. We can be obedient with a cheerful heart or grudgingly drag ourselves to obey. We all do much in Christian service not always with the right attitude, motivation, or "as unto the Lord," as we know we should.

But our self-centeredness plays into the much bigger picture of following His example. If I have planned an event that is very successful, and I received no thanks or praise for a job well done, what is my response? Do I praise God for how it ministered to people? Or do I harbor resentment, the whole effort leaving a bad taste in my mouth? Did I plan the event for my glory or God's?

Jesus never did anything for Himself, to serve Himself in any way. Everything must always be about others. If we are unhappy, crabby, or grouchy, we need to ask ourselves why. Is the reason for this state of mind because I was not served? We don't realize our unhappiness is tied up in "it's all about me." We are unaware most of the time that this is why we have no joy. We are like the spoiled child, always unhappy when everything isn't about us.

We must die to self. "For you died, and your life is now hidden with Christ in God" (Colossians 3:3). Every time we go to serve, even in the mundane duties of the day, we must ask ourselves, "Are we serving, or expecting to be served?" If this is true, then we will do what Jesus did—come only to serve.

THOUGHT FOR THE DAY

How much more, then, will the blood of Christ, who through the eternal Spirit offered himself unblemished to God, cleanse our consciences from acts that lead to death, so that we may serve the living God!

Hebrews 9:14

Father God, how blind I have been and how spoiled I am! May I ask myself, throughout my day, whether I come to serve or be served. May I follow in the Master's footsteps. Amen.

Have you found yourself grumpy because you weren't served today?

A SACRIFICIAL OFFERING

Therefore, I urge you, brothers and sisters, in view of God's mercy,
to offer your bodies as a living sacrifice, holy and pleasing to God—
this is your true and proper worship.

Romans 12:1

SOMETIMES I WONDER ABOUT ALL THE DIFFERENT LESSONS
to be learned from dramatic incidents in the Bible. As a parent, the
sacrifice of Isaac has always stood out to me: "Then God said, 'Take
your son, your only son, whom you love—Isaac—and go to the region
of Moriah. Sacrifice him there as a burnt offering on a mountain I will
show you'" (Genesis 22:2). How could Abraham take his beloved
son, Isaac, tie him to an altar and obediently prepare to sacrifice him?
He trusted that God would either raise his son from the dead or stop
him before he plunged the knife into the young man's chest. And,
Abraham obeyed.

But I have wondered about another person in this story—Isaac.
The Bible does not tell us his reaction to being tied up and placed on
the wood of the altar. Did he struggle? Did he cry out to his father in
terror of what was happening? Or did he totally trust his father? There
is no mention of Isaac protesting or struggling in any way. Amazing.

There have been many teachings on this dramatic story. One
reflects the sacrifice Jesus made for us. Just like God provided a ram

to take Isaac's place, God provided His Son, Jesus, to take our place on the cross.

We all have an "Isaac" we need to offer to God. It could be something very dear to our hearts. And after we let go of it, He may or may not take it from us. It could be a test, like it was for Abraham. What is my "Isaac"?

And then I could be the "Isaac." What kind of a struggle or fight would I put up? Would I trust my Heavenly Father? Would I be willing to be sacrificed to fulfill God's will—figuratively or literally?

These are questions we need to ponder. God may never call on me to make that kind of a sacrifice, but don't I still need to be willing, as either Abraham sacrificing or Isaac being the one sacrificed?

THOUGHT FOR THE DAY

My sacrifice, O, God is a broken spirit;
a broken and contrite heart you, God,
will not despise.

Psalm 51:17

Father God, it is very chilling to think You could call me to make a sacrifice like Abraham or Isaac. I don't know how I would react. I would like to think I would trust You completely, but I probably wouldn't. Show me now if there is an "Isaac" that You require me to give up to You as an offering. Amen.

THE KNOT
IN THE SOCK

Be kind and compassionate to one another, forgiving each other,
just as in Christ God forgave you.
Ephesians 4:32

THERE IS A CHILDREN'S STORY ABOUT A PRINCESS WHO
went to bed on top of a huge stack of mattresses. She could feel a pea
under all those mattresses and was not happy about it. After all, she
was a princess! I'm just like the princess in the children's story. For me,
it's that little knot in the sock at the end of the seam across my toes.
That knot rubs my little toe against the shoe, causing much discomfort.
At first, it is a slight irritation, but as the day wears on, it becomes
very uncomfortable. My husband doesn't understand this. He said,
"It sounds like a personal problem to me."

The pea under the mattress and the knot in the sock are like
other irritations I hang onto. It becomes a personal problem like my
husband said. I don't, or won't, forgive the person that irritated me,
and I have no intention of communicating in a loving manner why I'm
annoyed. I would rather collect each irritation and file it away like a
lawyer preparing his case to present to the judge and jury. Except for
me, they just pile up inside, damaging my relationship with that person
and causing a wedge between me and my God.

It might just be an issue that has nothing to do with what they
said or did, but something that I need to change about myself. I need

to ask myself if it is something I'm very defensive about. Maybe that's why I can't let it go. But then it grows into a grudge against that person, and they have no idea why I have become so cold toward them.

The forgiveness comes when I ask God to forgive me for holding something against a brother or sister—that is my problem, not theirs. I need to ask forgiveness of that person and communicate why I have pulled away from them.

Going to Scripture, I will always find guidance for making things right with my brothers and sisters. The apostle Paul tells us, "Therefore, as God's chosen people, holy and dearly loved, clothe yourselves with compassion, kindness, humility, gentleness and patience. Bear with each another and forgive one another, if any of you has a grievance against someone. Forgive as the Lord forgave you" (Colossians 3:12–13).

And the bottom line is what Jesus says. "But if you do not forgive, neither will your Father who is in heaven forgive your transgressions" (Mark 11:26, NASB).

THOUGHT FOR THE DAY

Give those irritations to Jesus.

Father God, You know how I stockpile those irritations. I know it hurts You. Show me the reason behind why I'm irritated. May I bring these irritations to You to make right. Thank You for your forgiveness. Amen.

NOTHING MORE

Whom have I in heaven but you?
And earth has nothing I desire but you.
Psalm 73:25

AT THIS MOMENT, HORRIFIC WINDS ARE SCREAMING AROUND my house. Reno has been declared a state of emergency in the early hours of this November morning. The wind caused electrical wires to spark, creating a wildfire that raged through dry brush, jumping here and there, destroying homes and everything in its path. Twenty-nine homes were damaged or destroyed. The wind blew south, but what if it had blown north, my direction? What if I had lost everything but my life? Then what would I do?

It seems as though we spend our whole lives wanting more. The *"if onlys"* fill our lives from childhood on. Even an infant knows there's more milk out there somewhere and demands it. Every stage of our lives follows the same pattern—more money, more space, more toys, more leisure time, etc. Do we ever get to a place in our lives when we can say, "No more!"?

As seniors, no matter what our circumstances may be, can we say, "I need nothing more"? We may indeed be at a place where we have needs, material and physical, that would make life easier. As Christians, the all-sufficiency of Christ fulfills all our needs and wants. Our spiritual journey brings us to a place where we see that striving after more of everything can begin to pale in the light of eternity. Then we truly can begin to see, believe, and live in the peace and contentment of a life abandoned to Jesus. Peter once told Jesus, "Lord, to whom shall we go? You have words of eternal life" (John 6:68).

If I lose everything in a fire, how would I respond? I pray I would totally fall on Him, continuing to put my trust in Him for whatever lies ahead. I need only Him, no matter what *nothing more!*

THOUGHT FOR THE DAY

In the morning when I rise, give me Jesus.
You can have all this world, but give me Jesus.
And when I am alone, give me Jesus.
You can have all this world, but give me Jesus.
And when I come to die, give me Jesus.
You can have all this world, but give me Jesus.
—Traditional Spiritual

Father, like Peter, to whom else would I go? In Jesus I have it all! Just give me Jesus. Amen.

ENOUGH

*Not that I speak from want, for I have learned to be content
in whatever circumstance that I am. I know how to get along with
humble means,
and I also know how to live in prosperity; in any and every
circumstance
I have learned the secret of being filled and going hungry, both of
having abundance
and suffering need. I can do all things through Him who
strengthens me.*

Philippians 4:11–13 NASB

WHEN DO I HAVE ENOUGH? AS A CHILD, I THOUGHT I NEVER
had enough dolls or doll clothes. As a teenager, I really needed more
of everything—clothes, my own room, friends, a car, and of course
a boyfriend. As young marrieds and then as young parents, we lived
paycheck to paycheck, barely squeaking by. And even on to the years
of working and raising a family, our needs were met, but there always
seemed not to be enough of something—a new car, a bigger house, or
time and money to travel.

Oswald Chambers says it this way, "There is only one Being who
can satisfy the last aching abyss of the human heart, and that is the
Lord Jesus Christ."

Glyn Evans writes, "If Christ is not enough, nothing is enough,
and I am doomed to eternal restlessness in that case."

Beth Moore states, "Blessed are those who need God enough to know Him enough to love Him enough to know He's enough."

I realize now, closing in on the age of eighty, how foolish those yearnings were for all I thought I didn't have enough of. Now I can say with Paul, I have learned to be content with whatever, wherever, and whenever. Even if I don't have my health, or I'm barely making ends meet, whatever the circumstances, I do have enough. I have the love of my husband, family, and friends and our precious times together. I have all my senses to enjoy God's magnificent creation. But even if I don't have these, I have my Jesus, and He is enough.

THOUGHT FOR THE DAY

Whom have I in heaven but you?
And earth has nothing I desire besides you.

Psalm 73:25

Jesus, my Lord and Savior, You will always be my everything. You are enough. Amen.

COFFEE

For whoever wants to save their life will lose it,
but whoever loses his life for me will save it.

Luke 9:24

ON OUR CAR TRAVELS, MY HUSBAND AND I STOP FOR COFFEE here and there. On one of our trips through the Southwest, we felt it was time for a coffee break and to stretch our legs. The town where we stopped was small—I mean really small—but they had a funky coffee hut. There was a sign on the wall stating this: "It's not that I'm addicted to coffee or anything. I just don't function without it." We had a good chuckle. But that sign spoke to me, and I realized that was me! As a senior, I have been drinking coffee for years. And it has all caught up with me in the form of acid reflux. Ugh. I can still drink coffee, but I must limit it to two cups a day and lay off it altogether once in a while. As a writer, the cup in the afternoon gives me a needed jolt to get going on the next chapter.

But the question becomes, do I need the coffee to function? Isn't that like saying, "Jesus, You are enough as long as I can have my cup of coffee to function"? Coffee seems like a small thing to become a stumbling block in my obedience to Jesus. But if He says for coffee to go, I will obey. But what about so many things in my life that have a hold on me? Simon and Andrew *immediately* left their fishing nets and followed Jesus when He called (Mark 1:16–18). They left everything and followed Him.

I want to be so in love with Jesus that I would not give a second thought if He asked me to sell everything, pack one small bag, and go—maybe like Abraham, not even knowing where I was going! And yes, if He said no more coffee, ever again, so be it.

THOUGHT FOR THE DAY

All to Jesus I surrender,
All to Him I freely give;
I will ever love and trust Him,
In His presence daily live.
—Judson W. Van DeVenter (1855–1939)

Abba Father, You know how we struggle to let go of our stuff. Please remind me every day that You are all I need to function in any situation. Amen.

Are you holding on to something that Jesus has asked you to surrender?

HEART LESSONS

A HEART CONDITION

Test me, LORD, and try me;
examine my heart and my mind

Psalm 26:2

"Batter My Heart"

Batter my heart, three-personed God; for You
As yet but knock, breathe, shine, and seek to mend;
That I may rise and stand, o'erthrow me, and bend
Your force, to break, blow, burn, and make me new.
I, like an usurped town, to another due,
Labor to admit You, but Oh, to no end!
Reason, Your viceroy in me, me should defend,
But it is captived, and proves weak or untrue.

Yet dearly I love You, and would be loved fain,
But I am betrothed unto Your enemy:
Divorce me, untie, or break that knot again,
Take me to You, imprison me, for I,
Except You enthrall me, never shall be free,
Never chaste, except you ravish me.
—John Donne (1573–1631)

"BATTER MY HEART," A SONNET BY JOHN DONNE, REFLECTS
a man's desire to get right with God. He cries out to the three-personed
God who is Father, Son, and Holy Spirit. He knows he is being sought

because God "seeks to mend." The language of this poem published in 1633 is old, but the meaning speaks to us today.

We ask why the poet wants his heart battered. Toward to the end of the poem, we read that he has been taken captive by the enemy. Donne has been betrothed to Satan and wants God to divorce him from God's enemy. When he uses the word "again," it is obvious he has been in this situation before. He has been untrue, but he says, "Yet I dearly love You."

The language of the battering shows the force he expects from this three-personed God. He will "break, blow, and burn" his heart that has been taken captive like a town. Donne asks to be "imprisoned" by God or else he will never be free. He uses the intimate wording of the bride and the bridegroom, by using the words "enthrall" and "ravish." He realizes God's love is perfect.

Oh, how I want the three-personed God to batter my heart until I am entirely His! I have been a captive to sin too many times. He must batter my heart to imprison me in Him so I will be free. But it is I who must invite God in to do the battering. He knocks, waiting to be invited in.

THOUGHT FOR THE DAY

I will give you a new heart and put a new spirit within you;
I will remove from you your heart of stone and give you a heart of flesh.

Ezekiel 36:26

Three-personed God, I invite You in to batter by heart until I am entirely Yours. Amen.

NOT MY GLORY

Therefore in Christ Jesus I have found reason
for boasting in things pertaining to God.
For I will not presume to speak of anything
except what Christ has accomplished through me

Romans 15:17–18a NASB

I HAVE MANY INTERESTS AND PASSIONS IN MY LIFE. MOST have been centered around music. I learned to read words and music notes simultaneously. My dad and uncle were jazz musicians and often rehearsed in our tiny living room, with the furniture moved out onto the lawn. Band, choirs, music degrees and teaching were what drove me for years. This was my way to serve the Lord.

But then God slowly changed my focus. He drew me into a writing group, waking in me an interest that had long been dormant. I felt God was leading me to write devotions and a novel that had a purpose. I prayed that these would bring healing to others through His Word.

Taking the course, "Perspectives on World Christian Movement," led me into missions—through short-term mission trips and serving as the mission deacon at my church. These roles became another way for me to serve Him.

But I began to notice how the passion for each one began to wane even after short periods of service. *What's wrong, God? Where is the passion, the devotion to serve You in whatever You've called me to do?*

I asked Him, and He answered. And I was shocked when He revealed to me that, in those places where I'd served, I'd done so to bring glory to myself, not Him! I learned that I can't serve Him in any way if there is even a hint of desire to bring glory to myself. When my focus is to bring Him the glory, out of that flows the excitement and joy of whatever He has called me to do.

THOUGHT FOR THE DAY

Let the one who boasts, boast in the Lord.

2 Corinthians 10:17

Father God, forgive me. I know I can do nothing without You. Remind me daily that my only goal is to bring You glory and enjoy You forever. Amen.

Does this speak to you? What is God saying to you?

GOD'S WORD

ALL

I will extol the LORD at all times;
His praise will always be on my lips.

Psalm 34:1

HAVE YOU EVER DONE A WORD STUDY IN SCRIPTURE? IT CAN be mind-boggling when you look through a concordance for a simple word like "all." There are pages and pages, 16 ½ in my concordance, where this word is found in the Bible. Such a simple word can pack so much meaning. You could also take this word and make various categories of how it is used in the Old and New Testaments—possibly positive and negative uses. The word "all" could become a dissertation for a PhD!

This word caught my attention first in the book of Colossians. The apostle Paul uses the word "all" thirty-two times in this short epistle. Paul says in Colossians 1:17, "He is before *all* things, and in Him *all* things hold together."

But then in some places in God's Word, we might not like the word "all" so much.

"Do *all* things without grumbling or disputing " (Philippians 2:14 NASB, emphasis added). And then there is this familiar proclamation, "And we know that in *all* things God works for the good of those who love him, who have been called according to his purpose" (Romans 8:28). And what about James 1:2–3? "Consider it *all* joy, my brethren, when you encounter various trials, knowing that the testing of your faith produces endurance" (NASB, emphasis added). It *all* comes down to God's Word. "*All* Scripture is God-breathed and is useful for teaching, rebuking, correcting and training in righteousness, so that the servant of God may be thoroughly equipped for every good work" (2 Timothy 3:16–17, emphasis added). "All" describes what Jesus has done for us in 1 Peter 3:18, "For Christ also died for sins once for *all*, the just for the unjust, so that He might bring us to God, having been put to death in the flesh, but made alive in the spirit" (NASB, emphasis added).

Many more verses in Scripture speak to us about that word "all" and the places where God is telling us—"all" means "all."

THOUGHT FOR THE DAY

*Love the LORD your God with all your heart
and with all your soul and with all your strength.*

Deuteronomy 6:5

Abba Father, may the word "all" jump out at me every time I read Your Word. Amen.

LET US

*Dear children, let us not love with words or speech
but with actions and in truth.*

1 John 3:18

OFTEN WHEN I'M READING THE BIBLE, I NOTICE CERTAIN words or phrases that are repeated. The other day, the words "let us" stood out to me. I went to my concordance to discover the places those two words are used in the New Testament. What spurred this search coincided with my pastor's sermon on Sunday. We are going through the book of Ephesians. His focus the last two Sundays has been on unity in the body of Christ—unity within the generations and unity with the whole body of believers—denominations aside.

The Scripture that started this process was Hebrews 10:22–24. In those three verses, "let us" is used three times. Verse 24 brings us to the subject of unity. "And *let us* consider how we may spur one another on toward love and good deeds" Another place that encourages unity is found in Romans 14:13: "Therefore *let us* stop passing judgment on one another." And another one is found in Galatians 6:9–10: "Therefore, as we have opportunity, *let us* do good to all people, especially to those who belong to the family of believers."

There are many other places in Scripture where we can find those two words—"let us." As a body of believers, we must stop every time we read those words and ask ourselves a question. Am I part of the "let us"? If I belong to Jesus, I must be aware of what I'm being called to do as part of the body. And it starts with Hebrews 12:1–2: "Therefore, since we are surrounded by such a great cloud of witnesses, *let us* throw off everything that hinders and the sin that so easily entangles us. And *let us* run with perseverance the race marked out for us, fixing our eyes on Jesus, the pioneer and perfecter of faith."

When God says, *let us* go, do and speak, I want always to be part of whatever the call is. It is a privilege and an honor to be counted among those for whom Jesus might be saying, "*Let us* go over to the other side" (Mark 4:35). Maybe it is the other side of the street, town, or world.

THOUGHT FOR THE DAY

Let us not become weary in doing good,
for at the proper time we will reap a harvest if we do not give up.

Galatians 6:9

Father God, alert me to those two words, "let us," and help me to ask You if they are for me to act on. Amen.

WHATEVER

And whatever you do, whether in word or deed, do all in the name of the Lord Jesus,
giving thanks to God the Father through him.
Colossians 3:17

"WHATEVER"—SUCH AN OVERUSED EXPRESSION THESE DAYS.
It may have started with the younger crowd, but we seniors have definitely taken it on. It has such a negative feel to it. The context and tone of voice in which we say it can speak volumes. We can flippantly say "whatever" and really mean that we don't care about you or your opinion. We become frustrated when something doesn't go our way, and we emphatically exclaim "whatever" as we mentally or physically slam the door. It is interesting how we can take a word, and over time, change its connotation. But God's Word generally uses "whatever" in a favorable light.

Many places in the Old Testament we read, "Do whatever He tells you to do" (NASB). This signifies a sign of surrender and trust. In Genesis 41:55, for example, Pharaoh instructs his people in the time of famine to go to Joseph: "Go to Joseph; whatever he says to you, you shall do" (NASB). King Solomon in Ecclesiastes 9:10a tells us, "Whatever your hand finds to do, do it with all your might . . ." This concept is echoed in Colossians 3:23 and 1 Corinthians 10:31. The "whatever" we say and do needs to be done or said all to the glory of God. Romans 15:4 says: "For whatever was written in earlier times was written for our instruction, so that through perseverance and encouragement of the Scriptures we might have hope" (NASB). And then there is Paul's all-encompassing verse in Philippians 4:8 that uses "whatever" six times to make a point!

THOUGHT FOR THE DAY

*Finally, brothers and sisters, whatever is true, whatever is noble,
whatever is right, whatever is pure, whatever is lovely,
whatever is admirable—if anything is excellent
or praiseworthy—think about such things.*

Philippians 4:8

Father God, the next time I think or use the word "whatever," may I "park" on these whatevers! Amen.

THREE SIXTEEN

For God so loved the world, that He gave His only begotten Son,
that whoever believes in Him shall not perish, but have eternal life.

John 3:16

OVER THE YEARS OF READING SCRIPTURE, I HAVE BEEN
struck by the many repetitions I see. One in particular is the fact
that several significant verses have the address of 3:16. Coincidence?
Chance? I don't think so. As the rabbis of old would say, "Everything
means something."

The very first is found in Genesis 3:16. God is communicating
to Eve the consequences of her sin. Her pain will be multiplied in
childbirth.

In Ecclesiastes 3:16, King Solomon shares what he has observed.
"Furthermore, I have seen under the sun that in the place of justice there
is wickedness, and in the place of righteousness there is wickedness."

James 3:16 states, "For where jealousy and selfish ambition exist,
there is disorder and every evil thing."

Revelation 3:16 definitely is one to heed! "So because you are
lukewarm—neither hot nor cold—I will spit you out of ny mouth."

In Joel 3:16, God's protection is revealed: "The Lord roars from
Zion And utters His voice from Jerusalem, And the heavens and the
earth tremble. But the Lord is a refuge for His people. And a strong-
hold to the sons of Israel."

God tells us who we are in I Corinthians 3:16: "Do you not
know that you are a temple of God, and that the Spirit of God dwells

in you?" And then He blesses us in Ephesians 3:14–21. "... that He would grant you, according to the riches of His glory, to be strengthened with power through His Spirit in the inner man ..." And another blessing is found in Colossians 3:16: "Let the Word of Christ richly dwell in you, with all wisdom, teaching and admonishing one another with psalms and hymns and spiritual songs, singing with thankfulness in your heart to God."

For guidance, II Timothy 3:16–17, which declares, God's Word is all we need for everything. I John 3:16 says that Jesus laid down His life for us and we ought to do the same for others.

One of my favorites is Zephaniah 3:16–17: "In that day it will be said to Jerusalem: 'Do not be afraid, O Zion; do not let your hands fall limp. The Lord your God is in your midst, a victorious warrior. He will exult over you with joy. He will be quiet in His love, He will rejoice over you with shouts of joy.'"

I Timothy 3:16 is all about Jesus: "By common confession, great is the mystery of godliness: He who was revealed in the flesh, Was vindicated by the Spirit, Seen by angels, Proclaimed among the nations, Believed on in the world, Taken up in glory."

Remember when you're reading Scripture to look for verses, numbers, and a multitude of other repeats. Everything means something!

THOUGHT FOR THE DAY

Now may the Lord of peace Himself continually grant you peace in every circumstance. The Lord be with you all!

2 Thessalonians 3:16

Father God, every number in Your Word is important. Help me to take notice. Amen.

(Other 3:16 verses: Exodus, Numbers, Proverbs, Joshua, Daniel, Matthew, Mark, Acts, II Corinthians, Galatians, Philippians, I Peter. All the verses in this devotion are in NASB).

PAIN

AFFLICTION

Turn to me and be gracious to me,
For I am lonely and afflicted.
Psalm 25:16

AFFLICTION CAN BE EMOTIONAL OR PHYSICAL, OR BOTH AT the same time. After the above verse, King David says to God in verse 17, "Turn to me and be gracious to me, for I am lonely and afflicted. Relieve the troubles of my heart and free me from my anguish." Reading the Psalms of David, we are aware of his emotional suffering. We all have suffered this way at one time or another. Maybe a betrayal of a close friend or spouse has devastated us and broken our hearts, sometimes even to the point of suffering physically.

The apostle Paul suffered both kinds of affliction. In 2 Corinthians 11, he tells about being beaten with rods, stoned, shipwrecked, sleepless and hungry. He was also deserted by friends, and his heart broke when some turned from Jesus.

For the longest time, I could not understand why God would allow His godly men and women to suffer in any way. They were all totally serving Him. But then one day I stumbled upon Psalm 119:67: "Before I was afflicted I went astray, but now I obey your word." Ouch! I have been blessed with good health for most of my life. But I had taken pride in thinking it was my doing and not God's blessing. Now in the latter years of my life, I have been afflicted. I know some of the things I suffer are because I live in a fallen world. I also know God allows physical afflictions to get my attention. Another verse from

Psalm 119:71 gives me an additional reason: "It was good for me to be afflicted so that I may learn your decrees." But the verse that really clarified this all to me was Psalm 119:75: "I know, O LORD, that your judgments are righteous, And that in faithfulness you have afflicted me." That verse blew my mind. Because God loves me so much, He wants to keep me close to Himself, like the Father He is. I am His child, and in His faithfulness, He will afflict me so that I will walk in deep closeness with Him.

THOUGHT FOR THE DAY

*Make us glad for as many days as you have afflicted us,
for as many years as we have seen trouble.*

Psalm 90:15

Abba Father, thank You for Your afflictions. I know they are necessary to keep me walking closely with You. I love You. Amen.

PAIN TO END PAIN

But I am afflicted and in pain; May Your salvation,
O God, set me securely on high.

Psalm 69:29 NASB

THERE ARE MANY TYPES OF PAIN. EMOTIONAL AND PHYSICAL pain can come from many different sources. Emotional pain could result from a loss or a betrayal. Physical pain could be classified from minor to constant, unbearable pain. But both emotional and physical pain, more often than not, will require suffering pain to end the pain.

In Psalm 69:4, David cries out the reason for his pain: "Those who hate me without a cause are more than the hairs of my head . . ." And he pleads with God, "Answer me, O Lord, for Your lovingkindness is good; According to the greatness of Your compassion, turn to me, and do not hide Your face from Your servant, For I am in distress; answer me quickly" (vs. 16–17 NASB). King David went through many seasons of emotional pain and stress, but those times drew him closer to God.

Physical pain often means we must endure physical pain to end the pain. I have had carpal tunnel surgery in both wrists. The pain and recovery of the surgery were not as painful as what I endured for years. I don't know why I waited so long to correct the problem! I have friends who have had torn rotator cuff or knee replacement surgeries who have suffered much pain. But right after surgery, the pain, physical therapy, and long recovery time were at times almost unbearable. I'm sure they wondered, "Is this really going to be better in the end?" On the other side of surgery and physical therapy, they said, "Yes, now I'm pain free."

We know some go through unbearable pain until Jesus takes them home. If they walk with God, they will tell you that all the suffering has brought them closer to Him. He has used them to bring others to the Lord, encouraging them through their times of pain.

As we age, it seems our times of pain increase as our bodies wear out. It can be a frustrating time when we can't do the things we used to do, or are going through physical or emotional pain. In these years, we have a God who created us to cling to and grow closer to Him. One way or another, "This too shall pass."

THOUGHT FOR THE DAY

For he wounds, but he also binds up;
he injures, but his hands also heal.

Job 5:18

God of all comfort, when I am in any kind of pain, I may not understand what You are doing, but I trust You to do a work in me through it. Amen.

DYING TO LIVE

For me, to live is Christ, and to die is gain.
Philippians 1:21

I CAN ONLY IMAGINE WHAT IT MUST BE LIKE TO FACE THE death of your child. And even more astounding is to have the presence of mind and the compassion to offer the organs of this beloved child to others. Many would not live without these life-sustaining gifts. They wait and wait, hoping for that specific organ to give them the chance to not only live but also to relieve whatever suffering and pain they are experiencing. The recipients are so very sorry that someone had to die so that they might live. But they are forever grateful to those who surrendered these precious organs.

When I look at my own life, I am amazed that the God of the universe would send His beloved Son, Jesus, to take on human pain and suffering—and to die for me! And the question becomes, why would He die for me? "For God so loved the world (*me*) that He gave His one and only Son, that whoever believes in Him should not perish, but have eternal life" (John 3:16).

If I don't believe in God, if Jesus is not my Lord and Savior, I am spiritually dead.

Jesus died carrying all my sins—past, present and future—on Him on that cross so that I might live. Jesus died so I might live, just like a person waiting to receive a life-giving organ. He rose from the dead and now lives forever.

But now I must die. As grapes must be crushed to bring forth wine, so I must be crushed as Jesus was crushed to bring forth life. This means I must give up my right to myself. I must die to myself. "For if we have been united with him in a death like his, we shall certainly also be united with him in a resurrection like his" (Romans 6:5).

I want to live now, fully in all the ways God has planned for me. Jesus said, "I come that they might have life, and have it to the full" (John 10:10). And I look forward to that glorious day when I will die—to live for all eternity with Him.

THOUGHT FOR THE DAY

Do you fear death?

Father God, thank You for sending Jesus to die so I might live—abundantly here, and forever with You. Amen.

EXTERNAL LESSONS

ORANGE CONES

For this God, is our God forever and ever;
he will be our guide even to the end.

Psalm 48:14

EVERYTHING NEEDS TO BE UPDATED THESE DAYS. THE RING road around our city is not exempt. Several miles in our part of town have been under construction for a very long time. Widening roads, new turn lanes, sidewalks, and walls are included in the plan. Our lives have been driving a maze of orange cones for many months. As much as we grumble about the cones, they are a warning and a needed guide through the construction zone.

God has provided orange cones for us as we journey through our time on earth. Scripture shows us the way to go in every decision we make. Sometimes the instruction is as obvious as the line of those bright orange cones. Other times we must search, eyes more alert, to find the way through. As the road signs direct us through the maze of cones, God's Word does the same through life.

Some of those signs we might see are:

ROAD CONSTRUCTION AHEAD "For I am confident of this very thing, that He who began a good work in you will perfect it until the day of Christ Jesus" (Philippians 1:6).

LANE ENDS MERGE RIGHT (LEFT) "The mind of man plans his way, but the Lord directs his steps" (Proverbs 16:9).

BE PREPARED TO STOP "Wait for the Lord; Be strong and let your heart take courage; Yes, wait for the Lord" (Psalm 27:14).

EXPECT DELAYS "Man's steps are ordained by the Lord, How then can man understand his way?" (Proverbs 20:24)

REDUCE SPEED "Heed instruction and be wise, and do not neglect it" (Proverbs 8:33).

DETOUR "Then we who are alive and remain will be caught up together with them in the clouds to meet the Lord in the air, and so we shall always be with the Lord" (1 Thessalonians 4:17).

DOUBLE FINES IN CONSTRUCTION ZONE "Do not be deceived, God is not mocked; for whatever a man sows, this he will also reap" (Galatians 6:7).

(Above Scripture verses in NASB.)

Once the road construction is done, we will benefit from it. The same can be said of God's work in us. We must follow those road signs and the path of orange cones He sets out for us each and every day.

THOUGHT FOR THE DAY

For I know the plans I have for you, declares the Lord,
plans to prosper you and not to harm you, plans to give you hope
and a future.

Jeremiah 29:11

Father God, keep me alert to Your "orange cones" so that each day I don't miss Your guidance. Amen.

What specific guidance has God's orange cones given you lately?

URGENT!

At once they left the nets and followed Him.
Mark 1:18

URGENT! ASAP! STAT!

What is urgent?

It may be because I'm a senior citizen, but it seems to me everything today is urgent. Why would everyone constantly be checking their phones? They are continually on their phones texting, messaging, or whatever. The phone may be in their pocket for a few minutes, but then it is whipped out and checked. If a response isn't needed, the phone goes back in the pocket. Or they are texting, talking while they walk. How often has there been a truly urgent message? And if there was an urgent message, could it get through? I realize the cell phone is here to stay and is very useful. But *really* . . . 24/7?

The addiction to the cell phone is quite disturbing. (And yes, we seniors can be just as addicted as the younger crowd.) Even on your phone, does God come first? Or are you on for many other different reasons? Maybe God has an urgent message for you. But can He get through?

If you read your Bible and devotionals—or listen to sermons and praise music on your phone—that's good. But if not, it might be a good thing to log exactly how many hours you are on your phone. Maybe a fast from using your phone for a few days is in order. But make sure you let everyone know so they don't freak out and think something has happened to you.

The book of Psalms has a suggestion to think about: "In the morning, LORD, you hear my voice; in the morning I lay my requests before you and wait expectantly" (Psalm 5:3).

As far as an urgent message goes, this one is right at the top: "I tell you, now is the time of God's favor, now is the day of salvation" (2 Corinthians 6:2c).

An urgent message? The word "now" is definitely emphasized—an urgent message that you would not want to miss. If you are a believer, be honest: Has your time with Him become almost nonexistent because of the lure of who and what is on your phone?

THOUGHT FOR THE DAY

No time for God is a scary place to be.

Father God, anything in my life can become an addiction. Please make me very aware when I have crossed the line, especially if I'm putting anything before You. Amen.

EXPECT DELAYS

Wait for the LORD; be strong, and take heart
and wait for the LORD.

Psalm 27:14

MY HUSBAND AND I TRAVEL A LOT. WHEN THE DAYS ON THE road are long, the last thing we want to see is a sign that says: "Road Construction, Expect Delays." Sometimes the waiting period is short. But other times it can be a half an hour or more. When the delay is long, it could be that God is saying, "Don't be in such a rush; take time to rest; enjoy the area around you. Get out of your car and visit with those ahead of or behind you." God may have a divine appointment in mind.

When we pray, we always want to hear from God immediately, or at least within a day or two. We want answers to our prayers now, not down the road in weeks, months, or years. And then there is that possibility we won't have an answer in our lifetime. Most of the time it seems God is saying to us to expect delays.

The Old Testament from Genesis to Malachi holds prophecies of a coming Redeemer and Messiah. Genesis 3:15 speaks of the One coming who will crush Satan. David, in Psalm 110:1 states, "The LORD says to my lord: Sit at my right hand until I make your enemies a footstool for your feet." In Isaiah 7:14, " The virgin will conceive and give birth to a son, and will call him Immanuel." And again in Isaiah 9:6, "For to us a child is born, a son is given, and the government will be on his shoulders. And he will be called Wonderful Counselor, Mighty

God, Everlasting Father, Prince of Peace." These are but a few of some six hundred prophecies through thousands of years before the coming of Jesus, our Lord and Savior.

From Malachi to Matthew, there was a delay of four hundred years during which God was silent. The prophecies were there, but God was saying, "Expect a delay!"

I don't know about you, but I am so thankful to be on this side of the Old Testament.

Jesus has come and saved me. He paid the price. I'm redeemed by the blood of the Lamb.

Now God seems to be saying for me to expect delays until Jesus comes again, whether to take us home through our death, or until He comes in the clouds to take us to be with Him forever.

THOUGHT FOR THE DAY

Look for a divine appointment in the next delay that God brings.

Father God, I am so impatient for things to happen. The delays of some prayers to be answered are the hardest to wait for. And yes, I'm praying for patience. Amen.

Can you recall a time when you were delayed, and you became part of a divine appointment?

RUSHING AHEAD

Guide me in your truth and teach me,
for you are God my Savior,
and my hope is in you all day long.

Psalm 25:5

RUSHING AHEAD! THE DAYS OF OUR LIVES SEEM TO BE JUST that . . . and oh what we miss in the rushing. As a senior citizen, I must keep my body moving. My exercise every day is a walk of thirty to sixty minutes. Most days it is just a duty—get it over with as soon as possible. The whole walk is focused on what I need to do as soon as I get home and for the rest of the day. I may have exercised my body, but what have I missed in that span of thirty minutes? I probably did not hear what God's direction was for the day since I was so intent on my own agenda, and I certainly would not have seen much of His creation. More important would be a missed divine appointment He had planned with a neighbor or a stranger who wasn't even on my radar.

Rushing ahead also affects the future beyond my walk. As a senior, my mind keeps focusing on something else . . . what, I don't know. But I do know that there is not much time left . . . ten, twenty years?

"Come now, you who say, 'Today or tomorrow, we shall go to such and such a city, and spend a year there and engage in business and make a profit.' Yet you do not know what your life will be like tomorrow. You are just a vapor that appears for a little while and then vanishes away" (James 4:13–14, NASB).

All I have is today, or this moment. It should be, and that is sufficient to fill me with His presence, guidance, and what He wants me to do and see in that moment. If I rush ahead either in action or thought, I will miss the *now* He has planned for me. "Teach us to number our days, that we may gain a heart of wisdom" (Psalm 90:12).

THOUGHT FOR THE DAY

Stop, pray, and listen!

Father God, I used to pray as I walked. What happened? Please guide every moment of my walk and my day. I don't want to miss You and Your plan for the day! Amen.

When was the last time you walked or just sat and listened for God?

WEIGHT LIFTING

Be careful, or your hearts will be weighted down
with carousing, drunkenness and the anxieties of life,
and that day will close on you suddenly like a trap.

Luke 21:34

NO PAIN, NO GAIN. IF YOU ARE INTO ANY TYPE OF PHYSICAL training, you hear that expression. It is true to a certain extent. When you weightlift, you must have a plan for building your stamina and strengthening your muscles. You don't just walk into the gym and try to lift a weight far beyond what your body can handle. It would prove destructive to your body, injuring you beyond repair. But if you have a good plan that moves you to a goal that is attainable, you will experience pain or strain as you build and strengthen muscles. As you strain in the gym lifting those weights, you gain strength to lift heavier weights in time.

Spiritually speaking, it is the same way with God as our Trainer. Oswald Chambers says this: "God does not give us an overcoming life: He gives us life as we overcome. The strain is the strength. If there is no strain, there is no strength." We are strengthened in our walk with each trial, testing, and crisis we go through.

The apostle Peter says this: "In all this you greatly rejoice, though now for a little while, if necessary, you may have had to suffer grief in all kinds of trials" 1 Peter 1:6 (NASB). I have always been amused by that "little while." Whenever we are in a trial, the cry is often, *When will this be over?* It seems like it has been going on forever. And then

I am stopped by the phrase, "if necessary," which I never noticed before. If God deems it *necessary* to put us through a trial, He will. Why? To strengthen our faith, our trust in Him.

The result promised to us is in 1 Peter 1:7: "These have come so that the proven genuineness of your faith—of greater worth than gold, which perishes even though refined by fire—may result in praise, glory and honor when Jesus Christ is revealed."

Will it be a trophy for lifting weights in a contest or having the King of Kings commend us?

THOUGHT FOR THE DAY

For our light and momentary troubles
are achieving for us an eternal glory
that outweighs them all.

2 Corinthians 4:17

Father God, God of all strength, may I strain for the strength You provide when You put me through a crisis, trial, and testing as You feel necessary. Amen.

How is God strengthening you today? Are you straining as He empowers you?

HE'S
GOT YOUR BACK

*See, I am sending an angel ahead of you to guard you along the way
and to bring you into the place I have prepared.*

Exodus 23:20

MY HUSBAND AND I TOOK A TWO-MONTH CROSS-COUNTRY trip with our trailer in 2017. We covered 8,800 miles and nineteen states, and we experienced parts of God's country we had never seen before. We desert dwellers from Nevada were fascinated by states that were so green or had watered forests. We saw more mowed grass than we had ever seen in our entire lives—grass that grew right down to the highway pavement. And we saw flowers of every color that dotted the roadsides. And then there was the blessing of museums, tourist train rides, and different cultures. For example, the carts and horses on the roads in Amish Lancaster County, Pennsylvania, were certainly unusual.

Every day was an adventure as we navigated highways, big cities and small towns, RV sites and just the unknown of what the day held. But one thing was very evident to us—God had our backs!

We always start any plan for a trip with prayer. Psalm 16:8 is a good beginning: "I keep my eyes on the LORD. With him at my right hand, I will not be shaken." We knew He was guiding us when we began to make reservations for our next stop, but there were no available sites for our trailer! We had forgotten about the Memorial

Day weekend. But God had us covered. A site at a Corp of Engineers campground opened up. It was one of the most beautiful campsites we experienced on this trip. The sites were spacious with green grass, huge trees, a sheltered area, and a walking trail through thick vegetation to cool off. God provided many special spots like this for us to stay for the night or for a few days.

God was beside us all through this journey. When we needed an oil change on our truck, we were given directions to a place to get it done and in a timely manner. The same thing happened when we had a leak in our tire. We were directed to the right place at the right time. This happened many, many times, especially when we were lost!

But one of the more obvious indications of His loving care was on one day when I was in pain and wondering how I was going to manage a day of travel. When we began the day's journey and entered the next town, there were signs to not one, but two urgent care facilities. The one we picked gave me loving care. The pharmacy we used was just down the street! In this incident, God was truly, so to speak, carrying me. Psalm 89:1 is my song: "I will sing of the LORD's great love forever; with my mouth I will make your faithfulness known though all generations."

Far too often, we don't realize that He is really with us. He is always before, beside, and behind us. He truly has our backs!

THOUGHT FOR THE DAY

You have enclosed me behind and before,
And laid Your hand upon me.

Psalm 139:5 NASB

Abba Father, like a good Father, You have been, and will continue to be, on all sides of me. I'm forever grateful. Amen.

How quickly we forget that Jesus is with us 24/7. Think back just in the last few months and ask God to show you when He went before you, when He was beside you, and when He was behind you. Make a list and add to it.

HISTORY

THE INVISIBLE CHURCH

Day after day, in the temple courts and from house to house, they never stopped
teaching and proclaiming the good news that Jesus is the Messiah.

Acts 5:42

BROUGHT BY THE SLAVE SHIPS, THE AFRICANS CAME TO America knowing nothing of this new culture that would be their home. What a shock it must have been to go from a basic tribal existence to a country where there were buildings, horses, wagons, backbreaking labor, and a strange language.

As the Africans adjusted to their new life and the language of their masters, they also learned much of their new culture by watching and listening. The only entertainment was their songs and dances. They made music with sticks, pails, clapping, stomping, and singing. The songs they created were important to their well-being as a singing slave was a good slave. Singing in rhythm as they worked, they were more productive.

During the days of slavery in the South, an invisible church emerged. The slaves heard the music and Bible stories as they listened outside the open windows of the churches. They then passed the stories on to their children and fellow slaves. Hearing the gospel opened their hearts to follow Jesus. Not having much hope for a future, their songs focused on the hereafter. Their Spirituals are rich with Scripture and trust in God. They took what God gave them and worshiped Him in their "invisible church" that could be anywhere, and everywhere. They would gather for worship in secret places. If caught, the punishment could be severe.

As we entered the twentieth century, our African brothers and sisters were not allowed in the churches of the "whites," much to our shame.

It strikes me that the invisible church of the African slaves is much like the churches of our brothers and sisters in persecuted churches around the world. Many must meet in secret and move from house to house, or place to place to be safe.

While we still can meet openly, let's pray for others who are not able to.

THOUGHT FOR THE DAY

Never take for granted freedom of worship.

Father God, I am so thankful I live where I can worship You unafraid. I know the day is coming when that will not be the case. Thank You for the Africans You drew to Yourself to become part of the family. Thank You for their example and their music that enriches our lives. Amen.

A few of the many thousands of Spirituals:
- "Go Tell it on the Mountain"
- "Ezekiel Saw the Wheel"
- "Swing Low, Sweet Chariot"
- "Dry Bones"
- "Were You There?"
- "A Little Talk With Jesus"
- "Bound for Canaan Land"
- "Give Me Jesus"
- "Go Down Moses"
- "Little David Play on Your Harp"
- "Mary Had a Baby"

ROUTE 66

Give careful thought to the paths for your feet
and be steadfast in all your ways.

Proverbs 4:26

ROUTE 66 IS A FAMOUS HISTORIC HIGHWAY THAT TRAVERSES many of the states in America. Many of us have probably traveled at least parts of it, aware or unaware of its notoriety. Old Route 66 is notated on today's maps, but very little of it can still be followed. (Unless, of course, you are watching Disney's movie *Cars*.) The original highway ran from Chicago to Santa Monica, traveling through the major cities of St. Louis, Tulsa, Oklahoma City, Amarillo, Albuquerque, Flagstaff, and Los Angeles. For those who wish to travel this historic highway, there are websites for finding details. And of course, there is a website to find all the memorabilia available to purchase.

A while back, when I turned sixty-six, I realized I was on my own "Route 66." But it wasn't a nostalgia type of trip; it was totally unchartered and, to some extent, unknown. Much like Old Testament Abraham, we think we know what is going to happen today, but God may have something completely different in mind.

But we do go on those trips backward in time. For instance, we might retrace steps of our school years through elementary, middle school, and high school. Another path we might follow would be remembering the towns and houses we have lived in and jobs we have held. And for those of us with children and grandchildren, we have many side roads to look back on. We all do this at times, definitely dwelling on the happy memories while quickly passing over the sad ones, or like the line from the song "Memories" . . . "we simply choose to forget."

As we travel on in the reality of the now, we must keep our eyes forward. It is not good to take too many of those nostalgia trips. We must trust God for each day of this route He has us on . . . now.

THOUGHT FOR THE DAY

See, I will create new heavens and a new earth.
The former things shall not be remembered, nor will they come to mind.
Isaiah 65:17

Father God, too often I go on those nostalgic trips missing what You have for me now that is new and fresh. Please keep me focused on You and the here and now. Amen.

SYMPHONY

... to declare Your lovingkindness in the morning,
And Your faithfulness by night,
With the ten-stringed lute, and with the harp,
With resounding music upon the lyre.

Psalm 92:2–3 NASB

SYMPHONIES GENERALLY HAVE FOUR MOVEMENTS. EACH one has a character all of its own. It will incorporate a different key, tempo, mood, and one or more melodies. There may or may not be snatches of the main melody in each movement, tying the whole symphony together. Composers through the years have taken the symphonic form, and in some cases, changed it drastically. There may be more than four movements with no breaks between each one. Gustav Mahler (1860–1911) is one of those composers who burst the structure of the symphony. His *Symphony No. 3* is ninety-four minutes long with a huge orchestra, chorus, and soloist, a masterpiece telling a story. His *Symphony No. 8* is called "Symphony of a Thousand" because of the enormous performing forces of both instruments and voices.

Each one of our lives is a symphony that God has created. Some lives are short, with only a few movements, and we wonder why God chose to make that symphony so brief. For those in their senior years, the last movement may be coming to an end, while for others, He is adding yet another part.

Thinking back over our lives is like listening to a familiar symphony—the times of crisis where the music was dramatic:

fortissimo, frenzied; the times of sorrow in a minor key; lamenting, lento; the times of joy: allegro, celebrating. Each day may be a continuation of a section, or it may be the start of the final movement of our symphony, or just the next one, new and fresh in its mood and melody.

We want all of our lives to be composed in major keys, cheerful and joyful. How boring and uninteresting! Some of the most beautiful movements in symphonies contain melodies in minor keys that are incredibly sad and sorrowful, and parts that are stormy and fortissimo, much like our lives. In between those movements of storm and stress, God slips in the calm and rest, restoring our souls for what comes next, whether furioso or tranquillo.

The symphony God composes in our lives is the most unbelievable musical masterpiece that tells our own unique story.

THOUGHT FOR THE DAY

Read Psalm 150, praising Him as the Creator of your life.

Father Creator, may each movement of my symphony reflect the music of Your glory and love in my life. Amen.

For those of you who have a musical background, create a four-movement symphony in words of God's working in your life.

REMEMBERING WHAT GOD HAS DONE

The LORD has done great things for us,
and we are filled with joy.

Psalm 126:3

MY HUSBAND AND I HAD A RATHER SCARY EXPERIENCE recently in one of our snowy mountain passes. The Sierra Nevada Mountains had been experiencing one storm after another. We were on our way over the infamous Donner Pass when a semi and trailer jackknifed in front of us. The truck driver and my husband both managed to stop just feet from each other. No one was hurt, but the truck driver's trailer was damaged. The first words out of my husband's mouth were, "Praise God."

As seniors, we have probably experienced several, if not many, crisis situations in our lives. After the crisis is over and things have settled down, we sometimes forget what God did in that particular situation. Or maybe we were not even aware at the time that God was in every part of it and its resolution. Adrenaline often kicks in, and we turn to our human ways to manage the crisis as best as we can. Even on the other side of the crisis, we still may not see that God had everything in His control.

I can't help thinking of Moses and all his trouble with the Hebrews in bringing them into the promised land. God parted the Red Sea, and then they crossed and watched their enemy drown before their eyes. How could they forget something like that? They saw miracle after miracle of God feeding and clothing them. And He led them by a cloud during the day and a pillar of fire through the night. Psalm 78 recalls much of the Hebrew's forgetfulness of what God had done for them: "They forgot what he had done, and the wonders he had shown them" (vs. 11).

I'm afraid as the years go by that we do the same when a difficulty comes. We turn to our own devices to "fix" it. We forget what God has done in the past. He is the Creator of all, in all and over all!

THOUGHT FOR THE DAY

I remember the days of long ago; I meditate on all your works and consider what your hands have done.

Psalm 143:5

Father God, please bring to my mind all You have done in my life, especially when I forget Your sovereignty and power to accomplish amazing things. Amen.

Ask God to remind you of all He has done for you—from the small to the unbelievable. Make a list. (It might turn into a book!)

ORDER INFORMATION

CPSIA information can be obtained
at www.ICGtesting.com
Printed in the USA
BVHW030453210322
631910BV00002B/164